THE
ABRAHAM
LINCOLN
BOOK OF
QUOTES

A COLLECTION OF SPEECHES,
QUOTATIONS, ESSAYS & ADVICE
FROM THE 16TH PRESIDENT
OF THE UNITED STATES

EDITED BY TRAVIS HELLSTROM

hatherleigh

Hatherleigh Press is committed to preserving and protecting the natural resources of the earth. Environmentally responsible and sustainable practices are embraced within the company's mission statement.

Visit us at www.hatherleighpress.com.

The Abraham Lincoln Book of Quotes

Text Copyright © 2023 Travis Hellstrom

Library of Congress Cataloging-in-Publication Data
is available.

ISBN: 978-1-57826-970-9

Cover Design by Carolyn Kasper

Printed in the United States

10 9 8 7 6 5 4 3 2 1

CONTENTS

INTRODUCTION

ABRAHAM LINCOLN was one of the great leaders and thinkers of our time. He served as the 16th President of the United States, led our nation through the American Civil War, succeeded in preserving the Union, abolished slavery, strengthened the federal government and modernized the U.S. economy. He is remembered today as both a martyr and hero of the United States and is often ranked among the very greatest presidents in American history.

Much of his writing, speeches, stories and humor continue to inspire us today, but it is often hard to know where to start when it comes to learning from this great man. In *The Abraham Lincoln Book of Quotes*, we have taken some of Lincoln's most loved wisdom and shared them here in short and easy-to-remember quotations. The language may be simple, but we trust you will find the wisdom of Abraham Lincoln to be as profound today as it was in his time.

Whether you are reading just one quote at a time or enjoying them all in one reading, we hope the wisdom of Abraham Lincoln is as helpful and powerful for you as it has been for us.

BEGINNINGS

All that I am or ever hope to be, I owe to my angel mother.

~

You have to do your own growing no matter how tall your grandfather was.

~

I'm a success today because I had a friend who believed in me and I didn't have the heart to let him down.

I can remember our life in Kentucky: the cabin, the stinted living, the sale of our possessions, and the journey with my father and mother to southern Indiana. It was pretty pinching times at first in Indiana, getting the cabin built and the clearing for the crops, but presently we got reasonably comfortable, and my father married again...My father had suffered greatly for want of an education, and he determined at an early day that I should be well educated. And what do you think he said his ideas of a good education were? We had an old, dog-eared arithmetic in our house, and father determined that somehow, or somehow else, I should cipher through that book.

—*Remark to Illinois lawyer Leonard Swett,*
Fall 1853

CHARACTER

Character is like a tree and reputation like a shadow. The shadow is what we think of it; the tree is the real thing.

Be sure you put your feet in the right place, then stand firm.

I never had a policy; I have just tried to do my very best each and every day.

Tact is the ability to describe others as they see themselves.

The surest way to reveal one's character is not through adversity but by giving them power.

We should be too big to take offense and too noble to give it.

Whatever you are, be a good one.

America will never be destroyed from the outside. If we falter and lose our freedoms, it will be because we destroyed ourselves.

I walk slowly, but I never walk backward.

You have to do your own growing no matter how tall your grandfather was.

Nearly all men can stand adversity, but if you want to test a man's character, give him power.

You cannot build character and courage by taking away people's initiative and independence. You cannot help people permanently by doing for them what they could and should do for themselves.

As the patriots of seventy-six did to the support of the Declaration of Independence, so to the support of the Constitution and Laws, let every American pledge his life, his property, and his sacred honor; let every man remember that to violate the law, is to trample on the blood of his father, and to tear the character of his own, and his children's liberty.

Commitment is what transforms a promise into a reality...Commitment is the stuff character is made of; the power to change the face of things. It is the daily triumph of integrity over skepticism.

I am not bound to win, but I am bound to be true. I am not bound to succeed, but I am bound to live up to what light I have.

I desire so to conduct the affairs of this administration that if at the end, when I come to lay down the reins of power, I have lost every other friend on earth, I shall at least have one friend left, and that friend shall be down inside of me.

I see in the near future a crisis approaching that unnerves me and causes me to tremble for the safety of my country...corporations have been enthroned and an era of corruption in high places will follow, and the money power of the country will endeavor to prolong its reign by working upon the prejudices of the people until all wealth is aggregated in a few hands and the Republic is destroyed.

It's not me who can't keep a secret. It's the people I tell that can't.

You cannot escape the responsibility of tomorrow by evading it today.

Nations do not die from invasion; they die from internal rottenness.

No man has a good enough memory to be a successful liar.

We the people are the rightful masters of both Congress and the courts, not to overthrow the Constitution but to overthrow the men who pervert the Constitution.

You cannot build character and courage by taking away people's initiative and independence.

Let every man remember that to violate the law, is to trample on the blood of his father, and to tear the character of his own, and his children's liberty.

The way for a young man to rise is to improve himself every way he can, never suspecting that anybody wishes to hinder him. Allow me to assure you that suspicion and jealousy never did help any man in any situation. There may sometimes be ungenerous attempts to keep a young man down; and they will succeed too, if he allows his mind to be diverted from its true channel to brood over the attempted injury. Cast about, and see if this feeling has not injured every person you have ever known to fall into it.

EDUCATION

A new book is like a friend that I have yet to meet.

I am slow to learn and slow to forget that which I have learned. My mind is like a piece of steel, very hard to scratch anything on it and almost impossible after you get it there to rub it out.

Books serve to show a man that those original thoughts of his aren't very new after all.

Books, and your capacity for understanding them, are just the same in all places.... Always bear in mind that your own resolution to succeed is more important than any other one thing.

My best friend is a person who will give me a book I have not read.

The things I want to know are in books.

My great concern is not whether you have failed, but whether you are content with your failure.

I am absent altogether too much to be a suitable instructor for a law-student. When a man has reached the age that Mr. Widner has, and has already been doing for himself, my judgment is, that he reads the books for himself without an instructor. That is precisely the way I came to the law.

My father, at the death of his father, was but six years of age; and he grew up, literally without education. He moved from Kentucky to what is now Spencer County, Indiana, in my eighth year. We reached our new home about the time the State came into the Union. It was a wild region, with many bears and other wild animals, still in the woods. There I grew up. There were some schools, so called; but no qualification was ever required of a teacher beyond readin', writin', and cipherin' to the Rule of Three. If a straggler supposed to understand latin happened to sojourn in the neighborhood, he was looked upon as a wizard. There was absolutely nothing to excite ambition for education. Of course when I came of age I did not know much. Still somehow, I could read, write, and cipher to the Rule of Three; but that was all. I have not been to school since. The little advance I now have upon this store of education, I have picked up from time to time under the pressure of necessity.

A capacity, and taste, for reading, gives access to whatever has already been discovered by others. It is the key, or one of the keys, to the already solved problems. And not only so. It gives a relish, and facility, for successfully pursuing the [yet] unsolved ones.

Get books, sit yourself down anywhere, and go to reading them yourself.

If you wish to be a lawyer, attach no consequence to the place you are in, or the person you are with; but get books, sit down anywhere, and go to reading for yourself. That will make a lawyer of you quicker than any other way.

Those who write clearly have readers, those who write obscurely have commentators.

I am a firm believer in the people. If given the truth, they can be depended upon to meet any national crisis. The great point is to bring them the real facts, and beer.

Education does not mean teaching people what they do not know. It means teaching them to behave as they do not behave.

Your good mother tells me you are feeling very badly in your new situation. Allow me to assure you it is a perfect certainty that you will, very soon, feel better—quite happy—if you only stick to the resolution you have taken to procure a military education. I am older than you, have felt badly myself, and know, what I tell you is true. Adhere to your purpose and you will soon feel as well as you ever did. On the contrary, if you falter, and give up, you will lose the power of keeping any resolution, and will regret it all your life.

I will learn, the opportunity will come.

By the 'mud-sill' theory it is assumed that labor and education are incompatible; and any practical combination of them impossible. According to that theory, a blind horse upon a tread-mill, is a perfect illustration of what a laborer should be all the better for being blind, that he could not tread out of place, or kick understandingly. According to that theory, the education of laborers, is not only useless, but pernicious, and dangerous. In fact, it is, in some sort, deemed a misfortune that laborers should have heads at all.

Education is the most powerful weapon which you can use to change the world.

I have scarcely felt greater pain in my life than on learning yesterday from Bob's letter, that you failed to enter Harvard University. And yet there is very little in it, if you will allow no feeling of discouragement to seize, and prey upon you. It is a certain truth, that you can enter, and graduate in, Harvard University; and having made the attempt, you must succeed in it. Must is the word.

For my part, I desire to see the time when education—and by its means, morality, sobriety, enterprise and industry—shall become much more general than at present, and should be gratified to have it in my power to contribute something to the advancement of any measure which might have a tendency to accelerate the happy period.

Education is the movement from darkness to light.

I know not how to aid you, save in the assurance of one of mature age, and much severe experience, that you can not fail, if you resolutely determine, that you will not.

The philosophy of the school room in one generation will be the philosophy of government in the next.

Mr. Clay's education, to the end of his life, was comparatively limited. I say to the end of his life, because I have understood that, from time to time, he added something to his education during the greater part of his whole life. Mr. Clay's lack of a more perfect early education, however it may be regretted generally, teaches at least one profitable lesson; it teaches that in this country, one can scarcely be so poor, but that, if he will, he can acquire sufficient education to get through the world respectably.

Every head should be cultivated.

The old general rule was that educated people did not perform manual labor. They managed to eat their bread, leaving the toil of producing it to the uneducated. This was not an insupportable evil to the working bees, so long as the class of drones remained very small. But now, especially in these free States, nearly all are educated- quite too nearly all, to leave the labor of the uneducated, in any wise adequate to the support of the whole. It follows from this that henceforth educated people must labor. Otherwise, education itself would become a positive and intolerable evil. No country can sustain, in idleness, more than a small percentage of its numbers. The great majority must labor at something productive.

No man was to be eulogized for what he did; or censured for what he did or did not do. All of us are the children of conditions, of circumstances, of environment, of education, of acquired habits and of heredity; moulding men as they are and will for ever be.

Upon the subject of education...I can only say that I view it as the most important subject which we as a people may be engaged in.

FAMILY

Nothing new here, except my marrying, which to me is a matter of profound wonder.

God must love the common man, he made so many of them.

Love is the chain whereby to bind a child to its parents.

My wife is as handsome as when she was a girl, and I, a poor nobody then, fell in love with her; and what is more, I have never fallen out.

~

The greatest lessons I have every learned were at my mother's knees...All that I am, or hope to be, I owe to my angel mother.

~

I have come to the conclusion never again to think of marrying, and for this reason, I can never be satisfied with anyone who would be blockhead enough to have me.

Abraham took an early start as a hunter, which was never much improved afterwards. A few days before the completion of his eighth year, in the absence of his father, a flock of wild turkeys approached the new log cabin, and Abraham with a rifle-gun standing inside, shot through a crack and killed one of them. He has never since pulled a trigger on any larger game.

Women are the only people I am afraid of who I never thought would hurt me.

I remember my mother's prayers and they have always followed me. They have clung to me all my life.

The worst thing you can do for those you love is the things they could and should do themselves.

Let reverence for the laws, be breathed by every American mother, to the lisping babe, that prattles on her lap—let it be taught in schools, in seminaries, and in colleges; let it be written in Primmers, spelling books, and in Almanacs; let it be preached from the pulpit, proclaimed in legislative halls, and enforced in courts of justice.

Marriage is neither heaven nor hell, it is simply purgatory.

It is my pleasure that my children are free—
happy and unrestrained by parental tyranny.

With the catching ends the pleasure of the
chase.

Whatever woman may cast her lot with mine,
should any ever do so, it is my intention to
do all in my power to make her happy and
contented; and there is nothing I can imagine
that would make me more unhappy than to
fail in the effort.

There is another old poet whose name I do not now remember who said, "Truth is the daughter of Time."

You already know I desire that neither Father or Mother shall be in want of any comfort either in health or sickness while they live.

HAPPINESS

Most folks are about as they make their minds up to be.

~

Every man's happiness is his own responsibility.

~

The greatest fine art of the future will be the making of a comfortable living from a small piece of land.

We can complain because rose bushes have thorns, or rejoice because thorn bushes have roses.

~~~

I agree with you, Mr. Chairman, that the working men are the basis of all governments, for the plain reason that they are the more numerous, and as you added that those were the sentiments of the gentlemen present, representing not only the working class, but citizens of other callings than those of the mechanic, I am happy to concur with you in these sentiments, not only of the native born citizens, but also of the Germans and foreigners from other countries.

I am slow to listen to criminations among friends, and never espouse their quarrels on either side. My sincere wish is that both sides will allow bygones to be bygones, and look to the present and future only.

I'm a success today because I had a friend who believed in me and I didn't have the heart to let him down.

If you would win a man to your cause first convince him that you are his sincere friend.

In this sad world of ours sorrow comes to all and it often comes with bitter agony. Perfect relief is not possible except with time. You cannot now believe that you will ever feel better. But this is not true. You are sure to be happy again. Knowing this, truly believing it will make you less miserable now. I have had enough experience to make this statement.

The leading rule for the lawyer, as for the man of every other calling, is diligence. Leave nothing for to-morrow which can be done to-day.

Let us hope that by the best cultivation of the physical world, beneath and around us; and the intellectual and moral world within us, we shall secure an individual, social and political prosperity and happiness, whose course shall be onward and upward, and which, while the earth endures, shall not pass away.

The better part of one's life consists of his friendships.

HARD WORK

Work, work, work, is the main thing.

Always bear in mind that your own resolution to succeed is more important than any one thing.

Great men are ordinary men with extra ordinary determination.

Half-finished work generally proves to be labor lost.

And I am glad to know that there is a system of labor—where the laborer can strike if he wants to! I would to God that such a system prevailed all over the world.

Determine that the thing can and shall be done and then ... find the way.

I am always for the man who wishes to work.

Beavers build houses; but they build them in nowise differently, or better now, than they did, five thousand years ago. Ants, and honey-bees, provide food for winter; but just in the same way they did, when Solomon referred the sluggard to them as patterns of prudence. Man is not the only animal who labors; but he is the only one who improves his workmanship.

And, inasmuch [as] most good things are produced by labor, it follows that all such things of right belong to those whose labor has produced them. But it has so happened in all ages of the world, that some have labored, and others have, without labor, enjoyed a large proportion of the fruits. This is wrong, and should not continue. To [secure] to each laborer the whole product of his labor, or as nearly as possible, is a most worthy object of any good government.

51

I appeal to all loyal citizens to favor, facilitate and aid this effort to maintain the honor, the integrity, and the existence of our National Union, and the perpetuity of popular government; and to redress wrongs already long enough endured.

I don't believe in a law to prevent a man from getting rich; it would do more harm than good. So while we do not propose any war upon capital, we do wish to allow the humblest man an equal chance to get rich with everybody else.

I will prepare and someday my chance will come.

Labor is the true standard of value.

The prudent, penniless beginner in the world, labors for wages awhile, saves a surplus with which to buy tools or land, for himself; then labors on his own account another while, and at length hires another new beginner to help him. This, say its advocates, is free labor-the just and generous, and prosperous system, which opens the way for all-gives hope to all, and energy, and progress, and improvement of condition to all.

Wanting to work is so rare a merit, that it should be encouraged.

If at any time all labor should cease, and all existing provisions be equally divided among the people, at the end of a single year there could scarcely be one human being left alive- all would have perished by want of subsistence.

If you intend to go to work there is no better place than right where you are; if you do not intend to go to work, you cannot get along anywhere.

Labor is the great source from which nearly all, if not all, human comforts and necessities are drawn.

Labor is prior to, and independent of, capital. Capital is only the fruit of labor, and could never have existed if labor had not first existed. Labor is the superior of capital, and deserves much the higher consideration.

It is most cheering and encouraging for me to know that in the efforts which I have made and am making for the restoration of a righteous peace to our country, I am upheld and sustained by the good wishes and prayers of God's people. No one is more deeply than myself aware that without His favor our highest wisdom is but as foolishness and that our most strenuous efforts would avail nothing in the shadow of His displeasure.

The world is agreed that labor is the source from which human wants are mainly supplied. There is no dispute upon this point.

My father taught me to work; he did not teach me to love it.

No country can sustain, in idleness, more than a small percentage of its numbers. The great majority must labor at something productive.

The probability that we may fall in the struggle ought not to deter us from the support of a cause we believe to be just; it shall not deter me.

The working men are the basis of all governments, for the plain reason that they are the most numerous.

Upon this subject, the habits of our whole species fall into three great classes- useful labor, useless labor and idleness. Of these the first only is meritorious; and to it all the products of labor rightfully belong; but the two latter, while they exist, are heavy pensioners upon the first, robbing it of a large portion of its just rights. The only remedy for this is to, as far as possible, drive useless labor and idleness out of existence.

HUMOR

With all the fearful strain that is upon me night and day, if I did not laugh I should die.

As a general rule, I abstain from reading reports of attacks upon myself, wishing not to be provoked by that to which I cannot properly offer an answer.

Common looking people are the best in the world: that is the reason the Lord makes so many of them.

No matter how much cats fight, there always seems to be plenty of kittens.

My dear fellow, I have no money, but if you will go with me to the light, I will give you my note.

> —Lincoln, addressing a gathering of newspaper editors and likening his position to that of a man attacked by a robber

I suppose you meant that it was all right if it was good for him, and all wrong if it was not. That reminds me of a story about a horse that was sold at the cross-roads near where I once lived. The horse was supposed to be fast, and quite a number of people were present at the time appointed for the sale. A small boy was employed to ride the horse backward and forward to exhibit his points. One of the would-be buyers followed the boy down the road and asked him confidentially if the horse had a splint. 'Well, mister,' said the boy, 'if it's good for him he has got it, but if it isn't good for him he hasn't.'

—Lincoln, in response to receiving a telegram from Secretary of War Edwin Stanton that simply read 'all right, go ahead'

It is not best to swap horses while crossing the river.

If I were two-faced, would I be wearing this one?

Everyone desires to live long, but no one would be old.

There are no bad pictures; that's just how your face looks sometimes.

"The President said the Army dwindled on the march like a shovelful of fleas pitched from one place to the other."

—From the diary of John Hay,
Lincoln's secretary

How many legs does a dog have if you call the tail a leg? Four. Calling a tail a leg doesn't make it a leg.

Well, I wish some of you would tell me the brand of whiskey that Grant drinks. I would like to send a barrel of it to my other generals.

If it were not for these stories, jokes, jests, I should die; they give vent—are the vents—of my moods and gloom.

That some achieve great success is proof to all that others can achieve it as well.

The Bible says somewhere that we are desperately selfish. I think we would have discovered that fact without the Bible.

I heard a good story while I was up in the country. Judge D was complimenting the landlord on the excellence of his beef. "I am surprised," he said, "that you have such good beef. You must have to kill a whole critter when you want any." "Yes," said the landlord, "we never kill less than a whole critter."

KINDNESS

He has a right to criticize, who has a heart to help.

⁓

Better give your path to a dog than be bitten by him in contesting for the right. Even killing the dog would not cure the bite.

⁓

Am I not destroying my enemies when I make friends of them?

Adhere to your purpose and you will soon feel as well as you ever did. On the contrary, if you falter, and give up, you will lose the power of keeping any resolution, and will regret it all your life.

For it has been said, all that a man hath will he give for his life; and while all contribute of their substance the soldier puts his life at stake, and often yields it up in his country's cause. The highest merit, then is due to the soldier.

He who sees cruelty and does nothing about it is himself cruel.

I am in favor of animal rights as well as human rights. That is the way of a whole human being.

To ease another's heartache is to forget one's own.

I care not much for a man's religion whose dog and cat are not the better for it.

I could not have slept that night if I had left that helpless little creature to perish on the ground.

I would rather be a little nobody, then to be an evil somebody.

Rules of living: Don't worry, eat three square meals a day, say your prayers, be courteous to your creditors, keep your digestion good, steer clear of biliousness, exercise, go slow and go easy. May be there are other things that your special case requires to make you happy, but my friend, these, I reckon, will give you a good life.

With Malice toward none, with charity for all, with firmness in the right, as God gives us to see the right, let us strive on to finish the work we are in, to bind up the nation's wounds.

LEADERSHIP

I am for those means which will give the greatest good to the greatest number.

What kills a skunk is the publicity it gives itself.

Beware of rashness, but with energy and sleepless vigilance go forward and give us victories.

An allusion has been made to the Homestead Law. I think it worthy of consideration, and that the wild lands of the country should be distributed so that every man should have the means and opportunity of benefitting his condition.

Any people anywhere, being inclined and having the power, have the right to rise up, and shake off the existing government, and form a new one that suits them better. This is a most valuable—a most sacred right—a right, which we hope and believe, is to liberate the world.

As I would not be a slave, so I would not be a master. This expresses my idea of democracy.

But let the past as nothing be. For the future my view is that the fight must go on.

Don't kneel to me, that is not right. You must kneel to God only, and thank Him for the liberty you will hereafter enjoy.

Important principles may, and must, be inflexible.

Every man is said to have his peculiar ambition. Whether it be true or not, I can say for one that I have no other so great as that of being truly esteemed of my fellow men, by rendering myself worthy of their esteem.

I affect no contempt for the high eminence he [Senator Stephen Douglas] has reached. So reached, that the oppressed of my species, might have shared with me in the elevation, I would rather stand on that eminence, than wear the richest crown that ever pressed a monarch's brow.

I do not doubt that our country will finally come through safe and undivided. But do not misunderstand me...I do not rely on the patriotism of our people...the bravery and devotion of the boys in blue...(or) the loyalty and skill of our generals...But the God of our fathers, Who raised up this country to be the refuge and asylum of the oppressed and downtrodden of all nations, will not let it perish now. I may not live to see it...I do not expect to see it, but God will bring us through safe.

Fondly do we hope, fervently do we pray, that this mighty scourge of war may speedily pass away.

I do the very best I can, I mean to keep going. If the end brings me out all right, then what is said against me won't matter. If I'm wrong, ten angels swearing I was right won't make a difference.

I have always wanted to deal with everyone I meet candidly and honestly. If I have made any assertion not warranted by facts, and it is pointed out to me, I will withdraw it cheerfully.

If once you forfeit the confidence of your fellow-citizens, you can never regain their respect and esteem.

If there is anything that a man can do well, I say let him do it. Give him a chance.

Nowhere in the world is presented a government of so much liberty and equality. To the humblest and poorest amongst us are held out the highest privileges and positions. The present moment finds me at the White House, yet there is as good a chance for your children as there was for my father's.

It is safe to assert that no government proper ever had a provision in its organic law for its own termination.

It is to deny, what the history of the world tells us is true, to suppose that men of ambition and talents will not continue to spring up amongst us. And, when they do, they will as naturally seek the gratification of their ruling passion, as others have so done before them.

Stand with anybody that stands right, stand with him while he is right and part with him when he goes wrong.

Truth is generally the best vindication against slander.

There is an important sense in which government is distinctive from administration. One is perpetual, the other is temporary and changeable. A man may be loyal to his government and yet oppose the particular principles and methods of administration.

The privilege of creating and issuing money is not only the supreme prerogative of government, but it is the government's greatest creative opportunity.

Twenty-two years ago, Judge [then-Senator Stephen] Douglas and I first became acquainted. We were both young then; he a trifle younger than I. Even then, we were both ambitious; I, perhaps, quite as much so as he. With me, the race of ambition has been a failure- a flat failure; with him it has been one of splendid success.

PEACE

On the whole, my impression is that mercy bears richer fruits than any other attribute.

Peace is a thing which a person must be willing to fight for.

There's no honorable way to kill, no gentle way to destroy. There is nothing good in war. Except its ending.

Allow the president to invade a neighboring nation, whenever he shall deem it necessary to repel an invasion, and you allow him to do so whenever he may choose to say he deems it necessary for such a purpose—and you allow him to make war at pleasure.

Avoid popularity if you would have peace.

Kings had always been involving and impoverishing their people in wars, pretending generally, if not always, that the good of the people was the object.

And I do further recommend to my fellow citizens aforesaid, that on that occasion they do reverently humble themselves in the dust, and from thence offer up penitent and fervent prayers and supplications to the great Disposer of events for a return of the inestimable blessings of peace, union, and harmony throughout the land which it has pleased him to assign as a dwelling-place for ourselves and for our posterity throughout all generations.

Ballots are the rightful and peaceful successors to bullets.

Discourage litigation. Persuade your neighbors to compromise whenever you can. As a peacemaker the lawyer has superior opportunity of being a good man. There will still be business enough.

Military glory—that attractive rainbow, that rises in showers of blood; that serpent's eye, that charms to destroy.

Much is being said about peace; and no man desires peace more ardently than I. Still I am yet unprepared to give up the Union for a peace which, so achieved, could not be of much duration.

Now, and ever, I shall do all in my power for peace, consistently with the maintenance of government.

The dogmas of the quiet past are inadequate to the stormy present. The occasion is piled high with difficulty, and we must rise to the occasion. We cannot escape history. We will be remembered in spite of ourselves. The fiery trial through which we pass will light us down in honor or dishonor, to the last generation. We shall nobly save, or meanly lose, our last best hope of Earth.

Thus let bygones be bygones. Let past differences, as nothing be.

We have been the recipients of the choicest bounties of Heaven; we have been preserved these many years in peace and prosperity; we have grown in numbers, wealth, and power as no other nation has ever grown.

The strongest bond of human sympathy outside the family relation should be one uniting working people of all nations and tongues and kindreds.

EMANCIPATION

F our score and seven years ago our fathers brought forth, on this continent, a new nation, conceived in Liberty, and dedicated to the proposition that all men are created equal.

I have always hated slavery, I think as much as any Abolitionist.

If slavery is not wrong, nothing is wrong.

I know there is a God, and that He hates injustice and slavery. I see the storm coming, and I know that his hand is in it. If He has a place and work for me—and I think He has—I believe I am ready.

This is a world of compensations; and he who would be no slave, must consent to have no slave.

My concern is not whether God is on our side; my greatest concern is to be on God's side, for God is always right.

A house divided against itself cannot stand. I believe this government cannot endure, permanently half slave and half free. I do not expect the Union to be dissolved—I do not expect the house to fall—but I do expect it will cease to be divided. It will become all one thing or all the other.

As labor is the common burden of our race, so the effort of some to shift their share of the burden onto the shoulders of others is the great durable curse of the race.

Our political problem now is, Can we as a nation continue together permanently—forever—half slave and half free?

I have always thought that all men should be free; but if any should be slaves, it should be first those who desire for themselves, and secondly those who desire it for others. Whenever I hear anyone arguing for slavery, I feel a strong impulse to see it tried on him personally.

Do the people of the South really entertain fears that a Republican administration would, directly, or indirectly, interfere with their slaves, or with them, about their slaves? If they do, I wish to assure you, as once a friend, and still, I hope, not an enemy, that there is no cause for such fears.

[Stephen Douglas] is blowing out the moral lights around us, when he contends that whoever wants slaves has a right to hold them; that he is penetrating, so far as lies in his power, the human soul, and eradicating the light of reason and the love of liberty, when he is in every possible way preparing the public mind, by his vast influence, for making the institution of slavery perpetual and national.

In the first place, I insist that our fathers did not make this nation half slave and half free, or part slave and part free. I insist that they found the institution of slavery existing here. They did not make it so, but they left it so because they knew of no way to get rid of it at that time.

We are a great empire. We are eighty years old. We stand at once the wonder and admiration of the whole world, and we must enquire what it is that has given us so much prosperity, and we shall understand that to give up that one thing would be to give up all future prosperity. This cause is that every man can make himself. It has been said that such a race of prosperity has been run nowhere else…we see a people who, while they boast of being free, keep their fellow beings in bondage.

We were proclaiming ourselves political hypocrites before the world, by thus fostering Human Slavery and proclaiming ourselves, at the same time, the sole friends of Human Freedom.

I do but quote from one of those speeches when I declare that I have no purpose, directly or indirectly, to interfere with the institution of slavery in the States where it exists. I believe I have no lawful right to do so, and I have no inclination to do so.

I think that one of the causes of these repeated failures is that our best and greatest men have greatly underestimated the size of this question (slavery). They have constantly brought forward small cures for great sores—plasters too small to cover the wound. That is one reason that all settlements have proved so temporary-so evanescent.

What I do say is, that no man is good enough to govern another man, without that other's consent. I say this is the leading principle—the sheet anchor of American republicanism.

My paramount object in this struggle is to save the Union, and is not either to save or to destroy slavery. If I could save the Union without freeing any slave I would do it, and if I could save it by freeing all the slaves I would do it; and if I could save it by freeing some and leaving others alone I would also do that. What I do about slavery, and the colored race, I do because I believe it helps to save the Union; and what I forbear, I forbear because I do not believe it would help to save the Union.

I hate it because of the monstrous injustice of slavery itself. I hate it because it deprives our republican example of its just influence in the world.

Slavery is founded on the selfishness of man's nature—opposition to it on his love of justice. These principles are in eternal antagonism; and when brought into collision so fiercely as slavery extension brings them, shocks and throes and convulsions must ceaselessly follow.

In 1841, you and I had together a tedious low-water trip, on a steamboat from Louisville to St. Louis. You may remember, as I well do, that from Louisville to the mouth of the Ohio there were, on board, ten or a dozen slaves, shackled together with irons. That sight was a continual torment to me; and I see something like it every time I touch the Ohio, or any other slave-border.

In giving freedom to the slave, we assure freedom to the free—honorable alike in what we give and what we preserve. We shall nobly save, or meanly lose, the last best hope of earth.

Let us discard all this quibbling about this man and the other man, this race and that race and the other race being inferior and therefore they must be placed in an inferior position. Let us discard all these things, and unite as one people throughout this land, until we shall once more stand up declaring that all men are created equal.

So I say in relation to the principle that all men are created equal, let it be as nearly reached as we can. If we cannot give freedom to every creature, let us do nothing that will impose slavery upon any other creature.

So plain that no one, high or low, ever does mistake it, except in a plainly selfish way; for although volume upon volume is written to prove slavery a very good thing, we never hear of the man who wishes to take the good of it, by being a slave himself.

While I have often said that all men out to be free, yet I would allow those colored persons to be slaves who want to be; and next to them those white persons who argue in favor of making other people slaves. I am in favor of giving an opportunity to such white men to try it on for themselves.

I never in my life, felt more certain that I was doing right than I do in signing this paper...If my name ever goes into history it will be for this act, and my whole soul is in it.

—Abraham Lincoln at the signing of the Emancipation Proclamation on January 1, 1863

SPIRITUALITY

When I do good, I feel good. When I do bad, I feel bad. That's my religion.

~

Let us have faith that right makes might, and in that faith, let us, to the end, dare to do our duty as we understand it.

~

Both read the same Bible and pray to the same God, and each invokes His aid against the other.

If I were to try to read, much less answer, all the attacks made on me, this shop might as well be closed for any other business. I do the very best I know how—the very best I can; and I mean to keep doing so until the end.

—*The Inner Life of Abraham Lincoln: Six Months at the White House* by Francis B. Carpenter

The Bible is not my book nor Christianity my profession. I could never give assent to the long, complicated statements of Christian dogma.

I turn, then, and look to the American people and to that God who has never forsaken them.

The will of God prevails. In great contests each party claims to act in accordance with the will of God. Both may be, and one must be wrong. God cannot be for and against the same thing at the same time.

We accepted this war for an object, a worthy object, and the war will end when that object is attained. Under God, I hope it never will until that time.

Let us diligently apply the means, never doubting that a just God, in his own good time, will give us the rightful result.

We must remember that the people of all the States are entitled to all the privileges and immunities of the citizen of the several States. We should bear this in mind, and act in such a way as to say nothing insulting or irritating. I would inculcate this idea, so that we may not, like Pharisees, set ourselves up to be better than other people.

And having thus chosen our course, without guile, and with pure purpose, let us renew our trust in God, and go forward without fear, and with manly hearts.

And while it has not pleased the Almighty to bless us with a return of peace, we can but press on, guided by the best light He gives, trusting that in His own good time, and wise way, all will yet be well.

At the beginning of the war, and for some time, the use of colored troops was not contemplated; and how the change of purpose was wrought, I will not now take time to explain. Upon a clear conviction of duty I resolved to turn that element of strength to account; and I am responsible for it to the American people, to the Christian world, to history, and on my final account to God.

But I must add that the U.S. government must not, as by this order, undertake to run the churches. When an individual, in a church or out of it, becomes dangerous to the public interest, he must be checked; but let the churches, as such take care of themselves. It will not do for the U.S. to appoint Trustees, Supervisors, or other agents for the churches.

Certainly there is no contending against the Will of God; but still there is some difficulty in ascertaining, and applying it, to particular cases.

Near eighty years ago we began by declaring that all men are created equal; but now from that beginning we have run down to the other declaration, that for *some* men to enslave *others* is a sacred right of self-government. These principles cannot stand together. They are as opposite as God and mammon; and whoever holds to the one, must despise the other.

Remembering that Peter denied his Lord with an oath, after most solemnly protesting that he never would, I will not swear I will make no committals; but I do think I will not.

While I am deeply sensible to the high compliment of a re-election; and duly grateful, as I trust, to Almighty God for having directed my countrymen to a right conclusion, as I think, for their own good, it adds nothing to my satisfaction that any other man may be disappointed or pained by the result.

WISDOM

Die when I may, I want it said of me by those who knew me best, that I always plucked a thistle and planted a flower where I thought a flower would grow.

Give me six hours to chop down a tree and I will spend the first four sharpening the axe.

You can tell the greatness of someone by what makes them angry.

No man ever got lost on a straight road.

The best thing about the future is that it comes one day at a time.

Honor to the soldier and sailor everywhere, who bravely bears his country's cause. Honor, also, to the citizen who cares for his brother in the field and serves, as he best can, the same cause.

I do not think much of a man who is not wiser today than he was yesterday.

I am rather inclined to silence, and whether that be wise or not, it is at least more unusual nowadays to find a man who can hold his tongue than to find one who cannot.

If you look for the bad in people expecting to find it, you surely will.

Life is hard but so very beautiful.

The best way to predict the future is to create it.

Let no feeling of discouragement prey upon you, and in the end you are sure to succeed.

In the end, it's not the years in your life that count. It's the life in your years.

It has been my experience that folks who have no vices have very few virtues.

SELECTED
SPEECHES

First Inaugural Address

March 4, 1861

Excerpt: Intelligence, patriotism, Christianity, and a firm reliance on Him, who has never yet forsaken this favored land, are still competent to adjust, in the best way, all our present difficulty. In *your* hands, my dissatisfied fellow-countrymen, and not in *mine*, is the momentous issue of civil war. The government will not assail *you*. You can have no conflict without being yourselves the aggressors. *You* have no oath registered in heaven to destroy the government, while *I* shall have the most solemn one to "preserve, protect, and defend it". I am loth to close. We are not enemies, but friends. We must not be enemies. Though passion may have strained, it must not break our bonds of affection. The mystic chords of memory, stretching from every battle-field, and patriot grave, to every living heart and hearthstone, all over this broad land, will yet swell the chorus of the Union, when again touched, as surely they will be, by the better angels of our nature.

In this address, the new president appealed to the "mystic chords of memory" and to "the better angels of our nature" to hold the nation together. Seeking to alleviate the "Apprehension [that] seems to exist among the Southern States," Lincoln pledged not to interfere with slavery in the South and pleaded with the Confederate states to reconcile with the North. Twenty times he used the word "Union." But he also sent a

clear message that he would not allow the Union to be peacefully dissolved. "We cannot separate," Lincoln declared, and "the Union ... will constitutionally defend, and maintain itself." Though he wished for a peaceful resolution to the conflicts between the North and the South, Lincoln made clear that the Union would not back down if provoked and would not condone secession: "There needs to be no bloodshed or violence; and there shall be none, unless it be forced upon the national authority."

Six weeks later, the Confederates fired on Fort Sumter in Charleston, South Carolina, and the Civil War began.

The Gettysburg Address

November 19, 1863

Four score and seven years ago our fathers brought forth, on this continent, a new nation, conceived in liberty, and dedicated to the proposition that all men are created equal. Now we are engaged in a great civil war, testing whether that nation, or any nation so conceived, and so dedicated, can long endure. We are met on a great battle-field of that war. We have come to dedicate a portion of that field, as a final resting-place for those who here gave their lives, that that nation might live.

It is altogether fitting and proper that we should do this.

But, in a larger sense, we cannot dedicate, we cannot consecrate—we cannot hallow—this ground. The brave men, living and dead, who struggled here, have consecrated it far above our poor power to add or detract.

The world will little note, nor long remember what we say here, but it can never forget what they did here.

It is for us the living, rather, to be dedicated here to the unfinished work which they who fought here have thus far so nobly advanced. It is rather for us to be here dedicated to the great task remaining before us—that from these honored dead we take increased devotion to that cause for which they here gave the last full measure of devotion—that we here highly resolve that these dead shall not have died in vain—that this nation, under

God, shall have a new birth of freedom, and that government of the people, by the people, for the people, shall not perish from the earth.

Lincoln delivered one of the most famous speeches in United States history at the dedication of the Gettysburg National Cemetery on November 19, 1863. The victory of U.S. forces, which turned back a Confederate invasion, marked a turning point in the Civil War. The speech is engraved on the south interior wall of the Lincoln Memorial.

Second Inaugural Address

March 4, 1865

Fellow countrymen: at this second appearing to take the oath of the presidential office there is less occasion for an extended address than there was at the first. Then a statement somewhat in detail of a course to be pursued seemed fitting and proper. Now, at the expiration of four years during which public declarations have been constantly called forth on every point and phase of the great contest which still absorbs the attention and engrosses the energies of the nation little that is new could be presented. The progress of our arms, upon which all else chiefly depends is as well known to the public as to myself and it is I trust reasonably satisfactory and encouraging to all. With high hope for the future no prediction in regard to it is ventured.

One eighth of the whole population were colored slaves not distributed generally over the union but localized in the southern part of it. These slaves constituted a peculiar and powerful interest. All knew that this interest was somehow the cause of the war. To strengthen perpetuate and extend this interest was the object for which the insurgents would rend the Union even by war while the government claimed no right to do more than to restrict the territorial enlargement of it. Neither party expected for the war the magnitude or the duration which it has already attained. Neither anticipated that the cause of the conflict might cease with or even before the conflict itself should cease. Each looked for an easier triumph and a result less fundamental and astounding. Both read the same Bible and pray to the same God and each invokes His aid against the other. It may seem strange that any men should dare to ask a just God's assistance in wringing their bread from the sweat of other men's faces but let us judge not that we be not judged. The prayers of both could not be answered—that of neither has been answered fully. The Almighty has His own purposes. "Woe unto the world because of offenses for it must needs be that offenses come but woe to that man by whom the offense cometh." If we shall suppose that American slavery is one of those offenses which in the providence of God must needs come but which having continued through His appointed time He now wills to remove and that He gives to both North and South this terrible war as the woe due to those by whom the offense came shall we discern therein any departure from those divine attributes which the believers in a living God always ascribe to Him. Fondly do we hope—fervently do we pray—that this mighty scourge of war may speedily pass away. Yet, if God wills that it continue until all the wealth piled by the bondsman's two hundred and fifty years of unrequited toil shall be sunk and until every drop of blood drawn with the lash shall be paid by another drawn with the sword as was said three thousand years ago so still it must be said 'the judgments of the Lord are true and righteous altogether.'

On the occasion corresponding to this four years ago all thoughts were anxiously directed to an impending civil war. All dreaded it; all sought to avert it. While the inaugural address was being delivered from this place devoted altogether to saving the Union without war insurgent agents were in the city seeking to destroy it without war—seeking to dissolve the Union and divide effects by negotiation. Both parties deprecated war but one of them would make war rather than let the nation survive, and the other would accept war rather than let it perish. And the war came.

With malice toward none with charity for all with firmness in the right as God gives us to see the right let us strive on to finish the work we are in to bind up the nation's wounds, to care for him who shall have borne the battle and for his widow and his orphan—to do all which may achieve and cherish a just and lasting peace among ourselves and with all nations.

On March 4, 1865, only 41 days before his assassination, President Abraham Lincoln took the oath of office for the second time. Lincoln's second inaugural address previewed his plans for healing

a once-divided nation. The speech is engraved on the north interior wall of the Lincoln Memorial. Lincoln's Second Inaugural Address is heralded as one of the most significant presidential speeches in American history. Carved into the north wall of the Lincoln Memorial, its meaning and eloquence still resonate with people today. This speech packs a lot of meaning and yet, it is the second shortest second inaugural address in American Presidential history. Only George Washington's second inaugural speech was shorter (at 135 words compared to Lincoln's 703 words).

REFLECTIONS
ON LINCOLN

"Now, he belongs to the ages."
> —Edwin Stanton, Secretary of
> War and close friend of Lincoln,
> in the moments after he took his last
> breath as President Abraham Lincoln died
> in a first-floor bedroom at
> the Petersen Boarding House at
> 7:22 a.m. on April 15, 1865.

"It is the strangest and yet the fittest thing in the jumble of human vicissitudes, that he, out of so many millions, unlooked for, unselected by any intelligible process that could be based upon his genuine qualities, unknown to those who chose him, and unsuspected of what endowments may adapt him for his tremendous responsibility, should have found the way open for him to fling his lank personality into the chair of state—where, I presume, it was his first impulse to throw his legs on the council-table, and tell the Cabinet Ministers a story."

—Nathaniel Hawthorne, July 1862

"While Abraham Lincoln will not go down to posterity as Abraham the Great, or as Abraham the Wise, or as Abraham the Eloquent—although he is all three—wise, great, and eloquent he will go down to posterity if the country is saved, as Honest Abraham...and going down thus, his name may be written anywhere in this wide world of ours, side by side with that of Washington, without disparaging the latter."

—Frederick Douglass, December 4, 1863

"This dust was once the man,
Gentle, plain, just and resolute, under whose cautious hand,
Against the foulest crime in history known in any land or age,
Was saved the Union of these States.
Walt Whitman, Memories of President Lincoln, This Dust Was Once the Man

O Captain! My Captain! our fearful trip
is done;
The ship has weather'd every rack, the prize
we sought is won;
The port is near, the bells I hear, the people
all exulting,
While follow eyes the steady keel, the vessel
grim and daring:
But O heart! heart! heart!
O the bleeding drops of red,
Where on the deck my Captain lies,
Fallen cold and dead.

O Captain! My Captain! rise up and hear the
bells;

Rise up—for you the flag is flung—for you
the bugle trills;

For you bouquets and ribbon'd wreaths—for
you the shores a-crowding;

For you they call, the swaying mass, their
eager faces turning;

Here captain! dear father!

This arm beneath your head;

It is some dream that on the deck,

You've fallen cold and dead.

My Captain does not answer, his lips are pale
and still;

My father does not feel my arm, he has no
pulse nor will;

The ship is anchor'd safe and sound, its voy-
age closed and done;

From fearful trip, the victor ship, comes in
with object won;

Exult, O shores, and ring, O bells!

But I, with mournful tread,

Walk the deck my captain lies,

Fallen cold and dead.

"O Captain! My Captain!" *is an extended metaphor poem written by Walt Whitman in 1865 about the death of U.S. president Abraham Lincoln.*

"Viewed from the genuine abolition ground, Mister Lincoln seemed tardy, cold, dull, and indifferent; but measuring him by the sentiment of his country, a sentiment he was bound as a statesman to consult, he was swift, zealous, radical, and determined. Though Mister Lincoln shared the prejudices of his white fellow-countrymen against the Negro, it is hardly necessary to say that in his heart of hearts he loathed and hated slavery...Timid men said before Mister Lincoln's inauguration, that we have seen the last president of the United States. A voice in influential quarters said, 'Let the Union slide'. Some said that a Union maintained by the sword was worthless. Others said a rebellion of eight million cannot be suppressed; but in the midst of all this tumult and timidity, and against all this, Abraham Lincoln was clear in his duty, and had an oath in heaven. He calmly and bravely heard the voice of doubt and fear all around him; but he had an oath in heaven, and there was not power enough on earth to make this honest boatman, backwoodsman, and broad-handed splitter of rails evade or violate that sacred oath....

"Surveying the end from the beginning, infinite wisdom has seldom sent any man into the world better fitted for his mission than Abraham Lincoln. His birth, his training, and his natural endowments, both mental and physical, were strongly in his favor. Born and reared among the lowly, a stranger to wealth and luxury, compelled to grapple single-handed with the flintiest hardships of life, from tender youth to sturdy manhood, he grew strong in the manly and heroic qualities demanded by the great mission to which he was called by the votes of his countrymen. The hard condition of his early life, which would have depressed and broken down weaker men, only gave greater life, vigor, and buoyancy to the heroic spirit of

Abraham Lincoln. He was ready for any kind and any quality of work. What other young men dreaded in the shape of toil, he took hold of with the utmost cheerfulness."

—Frederick Douglass, Oratory in Memory of Abraham Lincoln (April 14, 1876)

"Once he called upon General McClellan, and the President went over to the General's house—a process which I assure you has been reversed long since—and General McClellan decided he did not want to see the President, and went to bed. Lincoln's friends criticized him severely for allowing a mere General to treat him that way. And he said, "All I want out of General McClellan is a victory, and if to hold his horse will bring it, I will gladly hold his horse."

—Dwight D. Eisenhower, "Remarks at the Birthplace of Abraham Lincoln", Hodgenville, Kentucky (April 23, 1954)

"When Abraham Lincoln signed the Emancipation Proclamation it was not the act of an opportunistic politician issuing a hollow pronouncement to placate a pressure group. Our truly great presidents were tortured deep in their hearts by the race question. [...] Lincoln's torments are well known, his vacillations were facts. In the seething cauldron of '62 and '63 Lincoln was called the "Baboon President" in the North, and "coward", "assassin" and "savage" in the South. Yet he searched his way to the conclusions embodied in these words, "In giving freedom to the slave we assure freedom to the free, honorable alike in what we give and what we preserve." On this moral foundation he personally prepared the first draft of the Emancipation Proclamation, and to emphasize the decisiveness of his course he called his cabinet together and declared he was not seeking their advice as to its wisdom but only suggestions on subject matter. Lincoln achieved immortality because he issued the Emancipation Proclamation. His hesitation had not stayed his hand when historic necessity charted but one course. No President can be great, or even fit for office, if he attempts to accommodate to injustice to maintain his political balance."

—Martin Luther King, Jr., Emancipation Proclamation Centennial Address at the New York Civil War Centennial Commission's Emancipation Proclamation Observance, New York City, (September 12, 1962)

Of Lincoln's increasing religious views, Lincoln's widow, Mary Todd Lincoln, said, "A man, who never took the name of the Maker in vain, who always read his Bible diligently, who never failed to rely on God's promises and looked upon Him for protection, surely such a man as this, could not have been a disbeliever, or any other than what he was, a true Christian gentleman....From the time of the death of our little Edward, I believe my husband's heart was directed towards religion and as time passed on—when Mr. Lincoln became elevated to Office...then indeed to my knowledge—did his great heart go up daily, hourly, in prayer to God—for his sustaining power. When too—the overwhelming sorrow came upon us, our beautiful bright angelic boy, Willie was called away from us, to his Heavenly Home, with God's chastising hand upon us—he turned his heart to Christ."

"Five score years ago, a great American, in whose symbolic shadow we stand today, signed the Emancipation Proclamation. This momentous decree came as a great beacon light of hope to millions of Negro slaves who had been seared in the flames of withering injustice. It came as a joyous daybreak to end the long night of their captivity."

—Martin Luther King Jr., "I Have a Dream" speech at the Lincoln Memorial (August 28, 1963)

"In the evening, when Michelle and the girls have gone to bed, I sometimes walk down the hall to a room Abraham Lincoln used as his office. It contains an original copy of the Gettysburg address, written in Lincoln's own hand.

"I linger on these few words that have helped define our American experiment: "A new nation, conceived in liberty, and dedicated to the proposition that all men are created equal."

"Through the lines of weariness etched in his face, we know Lincoln grasped, perhaps more than anyone, the burdens required to give these words meaning. He knew that even a self-evident truth was not self-executing; that blood drawn by the lash was an affront to our ideals; that blood drawn by the sword was in painful service to those same ideals.

"He understood as well that our humble efforts, our individual ambitions, are ultimately not what matter; rather, it is through the accumulated toil and sacrifice of ordinary men and women—those like the soldiers who consecrated that battlefield—that this country is built, and freedom preserved. This quintessentially self-made man, fierce in his belief in honest work and the striving spirit at the heart of America, believed that it falls to each generation, collectively, to share in that toil and sacrifice.

"Through cold war and world war, through industrial revolutions and technological transformations, through movements for civil rights and women's rights and workers' rights and gay rights, we have. At times, social and economic change have strained our union. But Lincoln's words give us confidence that whatever trials await us, this nation and the freedom we cherish can, and shall, prevail."

> —Barack Obama on on the 150th anniversary of the Gettysburg Address (November 19, 2013)

"As remarkable as it may seem, in 1861 Lincoln spent more time out of the White House than he did in it. And the chances are good that if a Union soldier had enlisted early in the Civil War, he saw the president in person. Lincoln made it a point to personally inspect every state regiment of volunteers that passed through Washington D.C., on their way to the front; and early in the war they all passed through Washington, D.C. Lincoln was probably the most accessible chief executive the United States has ever known...John Nicolay and John Hay, his personal secretaries, reported that Lincoln spent 75 percent of his time meeting with people. No matter how busy the president was, he always seemed to find time for those who called on him."

—Donald T. Phillips, *Lincoln On Leadership: Executive Strategies for Tough Times*

I would give all I am worth, and go into debt, to be able to write so fine a piece as I think that is. Neither do I know who is the author. I met it in a straggling form in a newspaper last summer, and I remember to have seen it once before, about fifteen years ago, and this is all I know about it.

—Abraham Lincoln in a letter to a friend, Andrew Johnston

Lincoln is referring to a poem titled Mortality by William Knox. Lincoln memorized the entire poem and recited it so often that some folks mistakenly thought he was the author.

The lines of Mortality are as follows:

Oh, why should the spirit of mortal be proud?
Like a swift-fleeting meteor, a fast-flying cloud,
A flash of the lightning, a break of the wave,
He passes from life to his rest in the grave.

The leaves of the oak and the willow
shall fade,
Be scattered around, and together be laid;
And the young and the old, the low and
the high,
Shall molder to dust, and together shall lie.

The infant a mother attended and loved;
The mother that infant's affection who
proved;
The husband, that mother and infant who
blessed;
Each, all, are away to their dwelling of rest.

The maid on whose cheek, on whose brow, in
whose eye,
Shone beauty and pleasure - her triumphs
are by;
And the memory of those who loved her and
praised,
Are alike from the minds of the living erased.

The hand of the king that the sceptre hath
borne,
The brow of the priest that the mitre
hath worn,
The eye of the sage, and the heart of the
brave,
Are hidden and lost in the depths of the
grave.

The peasant, whose lot was to sow and to reap,
The herdsman, who climbed with his goats
up the steep,
The beggar, who wandered in search of his
bread,
Have faded away like the grass that we tread.

The saint, who enjoyed the communion of
Heaven,
The sinner, who dared to remain unforgiven,
The wise and the foolish, the guilty and just,
Have quietly mingled their bones in the dust.

So the multitude goes - like the flower or
the weed
That withers away to let others succeed;
So the multitude comes - even those we
behold,
To repeat every tale that has often been told.

For we are the same that our fathers
have been;
We see the same sights that our fathers
have seen;
We drink the same stream, we feel the
same sun,
And run the same course that our fathers
have run.

The thoughts we are thinking, our fathers
would think;
From the death we are shrinking, our fathers
would shrink;
To the life we are clinging, they also would
cling -
But it speeds from us all like a bird on
the wing.

They loved - but the story we cannot unfold;
They scorned - but the heart of the haughty
is cold;
They grieved - but no wail from their slumber
will come;
They joyed - but the tongue of their gladness
is dumb.

They died - aye, they died - we things that are now,
That walk on the turf that lies over their brow,
And make in their dwellings a transient abode,
Meet the things that they met on their pilgrimage road.

Yea, hope and despondency, pleasure and pain,
Are mingled together in sunshine and rain;
And the smile and the tear, the song and the dirge,
Still follow each other, like surge upon surge.

'Tis the wink of an eye - 'tis the draught of a breath -
From the blossom of health to the paleness of death,
From the gilded saloon to the bier and the shroud
Oh, why should the spirit of mortal be proud?

The items in Abraham Lincoln's pockets the night of his assassination were as follows: a pocketknife, a linen handkerchief embroidered A. Lincoln, a sleeve button, a watch fob, two pairs of spectacles, one with string replacing a hinge, a lens polisher, a tiny pencil, tiny fragments of hard red and green candy, a fine brownish powder which appeared to be snuff, and a brown leather wallet (one section was engraved "U.S. Currency" and another section was engraved "Notes"). The wallet contained only a Confederate five dollar bill, and nine old newspaper clippings. Included among these clippings were two articles of praise and five others dealing with the issues that were on Lincoln's mind during his final months. These items are now in the Library of Congress.

REFERENCES

To learn more about this book, including access to a detailed list of resources for the quotes, speeches and stories referenced in this work, please visit www.travishellstrom.com/lincoln.